LIVING WITH DEPRESSION

ABDO
Publishing Company

LIVING WITH DEPRESSION

by Carol Hand

Content Consultant
Jean Anthony, PhD, RN, Associate Professor
University of Cincinnati College of Nursing

LIVING WITH HEALTH CHALLENGES

CREDITS

Published by ABDO Publishing Company, PO Box 398166, Minneapolis, MN 55439. Copyright © 2014 by Abdo Consulting Group, Inc. International copyrights reserved in all countries. No part of this book may be reproduced in any form without written permission from the publisher. The Essential Library™ is a trademark and logo of ABDO Publishing Company.

Printed in the United States of America,
North Mankato, Minnesota
092013
012014

 THIS BOOK CONTAINS AT LEAST 10% RECYCLED MATERIALS.

Editor: Jenna Gleisner
Series Designer: Becky Daum

Photo credits: Elena Elisseeva/Shutterstock Images, cover, 3; Thinkstock, 8, 11, 20, 30, 46, 50, 55, 80; iStockphoto, 17, 68, 88, 94; Iakov Filimonov/Shutterstock Images, 23; Steve Debenport/iStockphoto, 28; Shutterstock Images, 33, 36, 63, 70; Michael Jay/iStockphoto, 40; Vanessa Jones/iStockphoto, 43; Diego Cervo/Shutterstock Images, 60; David Sacks/iStockphoto, 73; GWImages/Shutterstock Images, 77; Monkey Business Images/Shutterstock Images, 85, 92

Library of Congress Control Number: 2013945893

Cataloging-in-Publication Data

Hand, Carol.
 Living with depression / Carol Hand.
   p. cm. -- (Living with health challenges)
Includes bibliographical references and index.
ISBN 978-1-62403-243-1
1. Depression, Mental--Juvenile literature.   I. Title.
616.85--dc23

                                                                    2013945893

CONTENTS

EXPERT ADVICE

I have a master's degree in adult psychiatric nursing. I have done many years of nursing in a psychiatric facility. Over the past ten years—since earning my PhD—I have taught and served nursing students in their psychiatric nursing training.

Throughout my work, I have noted that most frequently, teenage depression, specifically, is associated with drug use, family problems, and bullying. If I were to give any advice to teenagers living with depression, it would be this:

Depression is treatable. Know that there are places to turn and medication that can help you successfully handle your depression.

Seek help. Talk to someone, and do not try to handle it alone.

Try to picture depression as a unique opportunity. Depression offers you the opportunity to learn some invaluable, lifelong coping skills. These skills you will acquire will help you cope with and live with your depression as well as enhance your life by preparing you for future scenarios.

Try to be confident. You are not alone in your depression, and the fact that you are seeking help for it is a sign of strength!

While parents need to develop relationships with their teens, encourage their teens, and talk with their teens, teens also need to put a step forward and take control of their own situations. You should know that you can express your thoughts and feelings to your parents without being chastised or diminished. It's also important to note that technology alone cannot help you. Electronics and social media cannot take the place of your parents or other people in confiding in others for help and support.

—*Jean Anthony, PhD, RN, Associate Professor*
University of Cincinnati College of Nursing

HOW DO I KNOW IT'S DEPRESSION?

Ben walked down the school hallway with his head down, listening to the music in his headphones. People jostled past him, but he felt alone. He didn't know what was happening to him or why nothing seemed to matter anymore. He plowed headlong into

Suffering from depression can feel as if you're all alone. Coming to terms with your depression can help you work toward a happier life.

Mr. Hakim, his chemistry teacher. Mr. Hakim steadied him and took a closer look. "What's wrong, Ben?" he asked. "You look like you've lost your last friend."

Ben shook his head. "Nothing. I'm fine," he mumbled, and tried to push past. But Mr. Hakim persisted. "Let's go to my office and talk," he said.

Mr. Hakim told Ben this wasn't the first time he'd noticed Ben's sadness. He had seen other changes in Ben's personality, too. Last year, Ben seemed happy. He was always busy and part of a group. But now he was always alone. "You've lost interest in your schoolwork, too," Mr. Hakim said. "When you didn't turn in your last lab report, you just said, 'I didn't get around to it.' That's not like you—you've always been a dedicated student. What's going on?"

Ben shrugged. "I don't know," he said. "I just don't feel like doing anything. Nothing seems to matter anymore." He shifted uncomfortably and looked toward the door. "I should go. I've got class."

"I'll give you an excuse," Mr. Hakim said. "Right now, we're going to see the counselor. You seem depressed. You need to talk to someone—the sooner the better."

Ben didn't say much to the counselor, but his depression was obvious. The counselor called his parents. Ben was embarrassed about causing such a fuss, but he also felt relief. Someone had noticed.

DEFINING DEPRESSION

Everyone occasionally feels sad and depressed. Sadness is natural. For example, when you have a fight with your best friend or you don't get a part in the school play, you may feel depressed. But when its cause is resolved— you make up with your friend or find another activity—this kind of depression fades. It is a normal mood state caused by a stressor in your life. It is not a medical condition.

But what if you're like Ben and your depression doesn't have an obvious cause? What if it goes on so long you begin to feel life isn't worth living? If you remain severely depressed for months and don't bounce back, if your self-esteem is low and you feel worthless, or if you feel constant irritability and anger, you may have clinical depression. This is a serious mood disorder—an illness—that does not get better on its own and requires treatment.

Clinical depression always includes sadness and a loss of self-esteem. It is related to, but different from, two other mood disorders.

It's normal for every teen to feel sad or down at times, but if your sadness has lasted for longer than a few weeks, you may be suffering from depression.

Anxiety is a mood state in which you feel a sense of insecurity or worry. Grief is pain over the loss of someone or something important to you. Either anxiety or grief, if unresolved, can lead to depression. Those who develop clinical depression are also at greater risk for anxiety.

DEPRESSION IS INCREASING

Depression is on the rise. Ten times more people have depression now than those born before World War II (1939–1945).[1] According to the World Health Organization, depression affects 350 million people around the world and is "the leading cause of disability worldwide in terms of years lost to disability." Worldwide, there are almost 1 million suicides per year (3,000 per day).[2] Other psychiatric illnesses, such as bipolar disorder and anxiety disorders, do not show similar increases. Genetic changes occur too slowly to explain the increase. Some people think modern society is too self-focused and lacks the family and community support found in traditional communities. For example, people of the Amish faith living in Amish communities, who do have such support, show almost no depression.[3] Poverty, lack of education, exposure to violence, and being female all increase the risk for depression.

Clinical depression is sometimes described as either melancholic or non-melancholic. The melancholic form is based on your chemical makeup, while the non-melancholic form is more dependent on outside factors interacting with personality type. Stressful life events are more likely to trigger depression in people with anxious, self-critical, rejection-sensitive, or shy personalities. Also, any type of clinical depression may be either a primary or secondary condition. It is a primary condition when it is the main problem and causes the most severe effects, and when it was the first problem to appear. Secondary depression results from an earlier primary cause—for example, anxiety, alcohol or drug abuse, or another medical condition. An episode of depression usually lasts six to eight months, and episodes can recur periodically. Girls suffer recurrent episodes more frequently than boys.

SYMPTOMS OF DEPRESSION

People with depression can show psychological, behavioral, and physical symptoms. Symptoms vary in severity and from person to person. Not everyone has all symptoms. But a psychiatrist who detects five or more symptoms will diagnose the person with depression. Psychological symptoms include feelings of sadness and worthlessness or of anger and irritability. Behavioral changes include loss of energy, changes in sleeping habits or appetite, use of alcohol or drugs, and withdrawal from friends and activities. Physical changes include body aches, headaches, and stomachaches.

Depression can also accompany other illnesses, including anxiety disorders, alcoholism, and life-threatening illnesses. In these cases, it is important to diagnose and treat the depression separately from the other condition. But because diagnosis of depression is based on subjective symptoms, it is sometimes difficult to distinguish between the psychiatric disorder, depression, and another medical disorder of which depression is a symptom.

TYPES OF DEPRESSION

According to the *Diagnostic and Statistical Manual of Mental Disorders, Fifth Edition* (*DSM-5*), the classification of mental health disorders released in May 2013, there are eight separate classifications of depressive disorders, four of which are described below. Major disorders include:

Major Depressive Disorder, Single and Recurrent Episodes: This disorder is so strong it is disabling and interferes with normal life. Sufferers may be unable to work, eat, sleep, or study. They may lose interest in once-enjoyable activities.

Persistent Depressive Disorder: This disorder combines two previously defined disorders (Dysthymia and Chronic Major Depressive Disorder), which differ only in degree. Symptoms are constant and long-term, but not completely disabling. At some point, the person may suffer from major depressive episodes.[4]

Disruptive Mood Dysregulation Disorder: This disorder is diagnosed in children up to age

18 who are constantly irritable and experience extreme uncontrolled behavior.

Premenstrual Dysphoric Disorder: This disorder occurs monthly in women during the week before the onset of menstruation and declines thereafter.[5]

In addition to depressive disorders, the *DSM-5* includes another category—Bipolar and Bipolar Related Disorders—which includes seven different subcategories. Bipolar disorder (formerly manic-depressive disorder) is characterized by alternating mood changes from extreme highs (manic states) to extreme lows (depressive states).[7]

SIGNS AND SYMPTOMS OF DEPRESSION

According to the American Psychiatric Association (APA), a person suffering a major depressive episode displays at least five of the following characteristics during a two-week period, one of which is either depressed mood or loss of interest or pleasure. The symptoms must be present nearly all day, every day.

- Depressed mood
- Noticeably diminished interest or pleasure in activities
- Significant changes in body weight and/or appetite
- Significant changes in sleep habits (too much or too little sleep)
- Noticeable agitation and restlessness
- Decrease in activity
- Fatigue or loss of energy
- Feelings of worthlessness or inappropriate guilt
- Lowered ability to think, concentrate, and make decisions
- Recurrent thoughts of death; suicidal thoughts or actions[6]

OTHER FORMS OF DEPRESSION

Forms of depression that are less typical or develop under unique circumstances include:

Psychotic depression: combines major depression with some form of psychosis, such as delusions or hallucinations

Seasonal Affective Disorder (SAD): depression occurs during winter and lifts during spring and summer; seems associated with lower light levels

CHILDHOOD, TEEN, AND ADULT DEPRESSION

Depression appears very different, depending on your age and gender. Adults show the characteristic symptoms listed by the APA. Adult women have feelings of sadness, worthlessness, and excessive guilt. Men may be very tired, have difficulty sleeping, and lose interest in activities. They become frustrated, irritable, angry, or even abusive. They may behave recklessly or turn to alcohol and drugs.

As a teen, you are much more likely than adults to display your depression as anger and irritability rather than sadness. You may often have unexplained headaches and stomachaches. Because you may feel worthless, you are extremely sensitive to criticism or failure. Teens also tend not to withdraw from people completely, as adults often do. Teens do

Many behaviors change when a person is suffering from depression. One clear sign is a loss of interest in activities you used to enjoy.

socialize less but may maintain at least some friendships. Sometimes, they begin to hang out with different people.

After a first bout of depression, teens may suffer from more physical illnesses, behavioral problems, and emotional dependence on others. Adolescent depression also carries over into adulthood. Even minor depression can lead to more severe episodes of adult depression. Depressed teens are two to three times more likely than nondepressed teens to suffer from depression when they grow into adults. Research seems to suggest each episode of depression stimulates the brain, making it more sensitive to whatever factors trigger the depression.

Depressed children may show prolonged sadness, lose interest in playing and games, or show uncharacteristic behaviors such as bullying or stealing. They may be overly tired and have disturbed sleep or bed-wetting. They may also complain of feeling sick, refuse to go to school, cling to their parents, or worry their parents may die.

If you have symptoms of depression, it is vital to seek help quickly. Although each episode of depression does eventually end, early treatment can greatly lessen your suffering. Getting help is even more vital because each new episode of depression can be more severe than the last.

STATISTICS ON TEEN DEPRESSION

- Up to 8 percent of adolescents suffer from depression during any one-year period.
- The average age of depression onset in teens is 15, and it is common in those ages 10 to 14.
- From ages 15 to 55, girls and women are approximately twice as likely as boys and men to be depressed.[8]
- Seventy percent of adolescents who suffer one episode of depression will have recurring episodes.[9]

ASK YOURSELF THIS

- *Do you have symptoms of depression? If so, what are they?*

- *Can you think of any triggering events for your depressive symptoms?*

- *Are other people noticing your depression? In what ways is it affecting your life?*

- *How long have you been depressed? Have you talked with anyone about your depression?*

- *Have you thought about getting help for your depression? How do you feel about getting help?*

HOW DID I GET THIS WAY?

Alicia was angry. Every little thing upset her, and her mother was particularly annoying. Right now, she wanted Alicia to vacuum, and Alicia just wanted to sit in her room and listen to her iPod.

Depression can cause feelings of anger. Often, these feelings are taken out on loved ones, such as close friends and family.

"It's about time you started helping out around here," her mother snapped. "I'm tired of doing everything. I don't have the luxury of lying around like a lazy brat." Alicia was stung by her mother's accusatory tone.

"Yeah?" Alicia retorted. "What about all those times you just lie around for weeks and sleep or veg out in front of the TV and act mean and depressed? Are you being a lazy brat when you do that? I'll bet that's why Dad left—he couldn't take your bad moods!"

Her mother's face crumpled, and she quickly left the room. Alicia felt guilty and knew she should apologize, but she didn't move. The fact was, she blamed her mother for her own personality. She was sure she'd inherited her mother's bad moods and negative attitudes. She was afraid she would always be like this, and no one would ever love her—anyone who got close would leave, just like Dad had left her and Mom.

Finally Alicia sighed, got up, and dragged out the vacuum. She knew she should do something to get out of this funk, but she had no idea what. It was obvious her mom wouldn't be any help—she had her own problems. She didn't want to admit these feelings to any of her friends.

DEPRESSION IN BOYS VERSUS GIRLS

While all teens are vulnerable to rapid changes in brain development, girls are particularly at risk. Girls tend to have a higher level of emotional sensitivity than boys, and this sensitivity develops earlier. By mid-adolescence, girls are more than twice as likely as boys to suffer from mood disorders, including depression. The first sign of depression is usually withdrawal from activities, followed by sadness or irritability and changes in sleep or eating patterns, energy level, and school performance.

DIFFICULT TO DISCERN

As Alicia was feeling her depression, she was also considering causes for it. What makes her the way she is? Given how widespread and serious depression is, we know surprisingly little about its root causes. The cause of a given person's depression is most often not a single factor but instead a combination of factors—genetic, physiological, environmental, and psychological. Genetics, brain chemicals called neurotransmitters, hormone imbalances, and, in some cases, childhood trauma or learned thought patterns all seem to be involved.

POSSIBLE CAUSES

We know depression has a genetic component; it runs in families. One study showed children

Depression can be genetic. If depression runs in your family, talk to your family members about it. Chances are they have dealt with your same feelings.

of parents who suffered from early onset depression (before age 16) were 13 times more likely to be depressed themselves.[1] This risk correlates more strongly with depressed mothers than fathers. If both parents are depressed, the risk of their child being depressed rises substantially—from 30 percent for one parent to 70 percent for both.[2] Twins provide further evidence: if one identical twin suffers from depression, the other is very likely to be depressed as well, even if the twins are raised apart from one another.

Several parts of the brain play a major part in depression. Two parts of the limbic system (the amygdala and hippocampus), deep inside the brain, are associated with strong emotions such as fear, anger, and pleasure. The amygdala becomes more active during depression and emotionally charged situations. The hippocampus, which processes long-term memories, may work with the amygdala later in life to recall emotions associated with earlier stressful experiences.

IS THERE A "DEPRESSION GENE"?

No "depression gene" has been identified, and scientists don't really think a single gene is responsible for depression. There is some evidence depression is inherited on the X chromosome. Females have two X chromosomes in each cell; males have one X and one Y. Thus, females receive two copies of any gene carried on the X chromosome. This may help explain why females are more likely than males to suffer depression. But in some cases, depression is also passed down from father to son, so inheritance on the X chromosome cannot be the only explanation. Research continues to identify genetic markers for depression.

Cells throughout the brain and nervous system communicate by means of chemicals called neurotransmitters. These chemicals carry nerve impulses, or signals, from one neuron (nerve cell) to another across tiny spaces between the neurons. The body makes more than 50 neurotransmitters, each with its own function. Some are excitatory; that is, they stimulate the next neuron and send the signal on. Others are inhibitory; they suppress the signal. Changes in neurotransmitter levels affect a person's mood. This can occur if a neuron releases too much or too little neurotransmitter, or if the receptor in the next neuron takes up too much or too little.

Often the cause of depression is described as an imbalance in neurotransmitters (too much or too little), but the situation is more complex. Various factors, including genetics, stress, and hormones, as well as neurotransmitters, interact to cause depression, and millions of chemical reactions are constantly occurring in the brain.

Hormones also influence certain kinds of depression. Premenstrual dysphoric disorder is associated with changes in female hormones and has the same symptoms as major depressive disorder, although

NEUROTRANSMITTERS INVOLVED IN DEPRESSION

- **Acetylcholine: enhances memory, aids learning and recall**
- **Serotonin: regulates sleep, appetite, and mood; inhibits pain**
- **Norepinephrine: may trigger anxiety; helps determine motivation and reward**
- **Dopamine: affects motivation, reward, and a person's ability to perceive reality**
- **Glutamate: involved in bipolar disorder and schizophrenia**
- **Gamma-aminobutyric acid (GABA): may decrease anxiety**

symptoms last for approximately only one week each month. Incorrect levels of hormones from the thyroid gland can sometimes produce symptoms of depression. In these cases, doctors use blood tests to distinguish between a hormone imbalance and depression. The hormone melatonin is produced by the pineal gland, a tiny gland embedded in the brain. It affects moods and the body's sleep-wake cycles and decreases with low light levels. It is one cause of the form of depression known as seasonal affective disorder (SAD).

Environmental factors may also cause brain changes that can later trigger depression.

FACTORS INCREASING DEPRESSION RISK

There are many factors believed to contribute to the increase of a person's risk of depression, including:

- Low self-esteem due to factors such as obesity, bullying, or academic problems
- Witnessing or suffering violence, including physical or sexual abuse
- Family conflict or dysfunction
- Stressful life events, such as divorce, death, or a parent in the military
- Personality traits, such as pessimism or extreme dependence on other people
- Having another medical condition, such as anxiety, ADHD, or cancer
- Lacking friends or personal relationships
- Smoking or abuse of alcohol or other drugs
- Being female
- Being lesbian, gay, bisexual, or transgender (LGBT)

These factors include childhood trauma, such as physical or emotional abuse or losing a parent. Also, children can learn negative thinking patterns from parents or other adults. They may learn to feel helpless and unable to solve problems, which then leads to depression. Many psychological and environmental factors can also increase the risk of developing depression in people already genetically predisposed to it.

EFFECTS OF ADOLESCENCE

Depression affects teens and adults differently. Teen brains are still developing; they are not fully mature until a person's early 20s. During your teen years, you are at peak mental capacity but also highly vulnerable. Teens respond much more strongly than adults to emotional situations. Rapid changes in reproductive hormone levels affect sexual growth and behavior and social behavior. The hormone systems involved in stress reactions are also changing. Together, these hormonal changes have complex effects on behavior. Changes in regions of the brain that regulate the ability to sleep also occur during adolescence. These changes often lead to sleep deprivation, which in turn leads to depression and irritability.

In addition to the effects of rapid brain development, society constantly bombards adolescents with stressors. These stressors can

Some short-term stressors, such as pressure from a coach, teacher, or parent to perform a certain way, can contribute to your depression.

either be acute, such as pressure to pass a test or win a game, or chronic, which can vary from family pressure to excel to living in a violent neighborhood. Advertisers push unrealistic standards of beauty and body image, which teens struggle to meet. The news is filled with stress-inducing reports on the environment, crime, and war. Often, teens fight these stressors (and the depression they may bring) by trying to escape. They may abuse drugs or alcohol or withdraw into the virtual world of the Internet.

Many factors can contribute to depression, but usually the cause is a combination of several factors. Some factors are beyond your control—your genes, for example. But you have the power to control, reduce, or change many of them. Doing this can help you control or reduce your depression.

ASK YOURSELF THIS

- *Can you define factors that might be causing your depression?*

- *Do you have family members who suffer from depression? How have they handled their depression?*

- *Can you identify any risk factors in your life that may increase your depression? It so, what can you do to change these factors?*

- *Do you think your depression will get better as you grow up and your brain becomes completely developed? Why or why not?*

- *Do you use any behaviors to try to avoid or escape your depression? If so, what are they? Do you think escaping is a good idea? Why or why not?*

WHAT CAN HAPPEN TO ME?

Jamil walked out the front door after school, lugging his heavy backpack. He was not paying attention: he was brooding about the two midterms he was sure he had just flunked. Suddenly, someone shoved him down the steps. He hit his head on the concrete and lay there, stunned. When he could focus again, he saw Derek, Matt, and Tyler standing over him, grinning. Several other students came over to watch. He heard laughter and jeering.

"Hey, loser, why don't you watch where you're going?" Derek said it loudly so everyone could hear. Jamil's head hurt and he felt bruised all over. He tried to get up, but Tyler kicked him hard in the ribs. He curled up and covered his face, both to protect it and to hide his humiliation.

Jamil knew they would get bored and leave if he didn't react. But Derek wasn't finished. "Creep!" he taunted. "You'd better keep that geeky backpack out of people's way. We don't need your kind around here! Why don't you go back to the desert?" He gave Jamil a final kick and they all left, still laughing. The crowd broke up. No one helped him as he crawled to his feet and limped toward home.

This had been Jamil's life since he started high school—bullies, failure, and crude insults about his Middle Eastern heritage. *He's right, I am a loser,* he thought. Jamil felt he didn't have a chance at this school. And lately, he couldn't even be proud of his schoolwork. His parents would kill him. Grades were all they cared about.

Before walking home, Jamil stopped at the park to think. He wondered how long he could go on like this. Lately, he'd been thinking a lot about killing himself, and the idea was looking better all the time.

WHAT CAN HAPPEN?

Jamil is severely depressed, and stresses at school are deepening his depression. As his case illustrates, depression is a serious illness and can lead to many complications—some life threatening. Depression can be treated very successfully. But what are the consequences of not dealing with it? If you choose not

BULLYING AND DEPRESSION

Teens seen as "different" are at greater risk of bullying. Groups targeted for bullying often include the disabled, those with a different religion, those of a different race, and lesbian, gay, bisexual, or transgender teens. Bullying may be based on misinformation or negative perceptions of a group; for example, associating all Muslims with terrorist activity. Outward symbols of a group, such as a Muslim girl wearing a hijab, may trigger bullying.

Bullied teens suffer many symptoms of depression and anxiety. They are sad and lonely, and they lose interest in activities. They have more health complaints. Their schoolwork suffers, and they may skip school or drop out. A very few may retaliate violently. During the 1990s, students who had been bullied carried out 12 of 15 school shootings.[1]

Bullying by itself does not cause suicide, but it can make an already depressed teen more prone to thoughts of suicide.

to address your depression, your grades and relationships with friends and family may start to suffer. It's possible you may turn to drugs and alcohol; and, even worse, if you don't address your depression for too long, you could begin to have thoughts of suicide.

ACADEMIC PROBLEMS

Depression almost inevitably leads to academic problems. Depressed teens have trouble thinking and concentrating. You may find it difficult or impossible to complete assignments, or maybe you think it's not worth the effort. So you miss classes or cut school. You may give up more easily, be afraid to tackle difficult assignments, or have a low tolerance for frustration. Depression correlates strongly with poor school performance, and the more depressed you are, the more likely you are to drop out of school.

FAMILY AND RELATIONSHIP PROBLEMS

Depression makes it harder for depressed teens to maintain healthy relationships. Depression may take different forms in different people, making it difficult to identify. One teen may seem to handle serious stressors very well, and his family doesn't recognize his depression until he tries to commit suicide. Another may lash out, be defiant, have violent outbursts, and fight with parents and siblings. These teens express their depression in very different ways, but

LOW SELF-ESTEEM

Stressful life events by themselves do not cause depression, but they strongly interact with low self-esteem. Low self-esteem seems to make people more prone to depression by lowering their tolerance to handle stressful events. This can happen when a teen is constantly bullied, humiliated, belittled, or isolated. If the stress continues for a long time, the person loses the ability to spring back. Constant trampling of self-esteem can trigger depressive episodes or deepen existing depression.

neither confides their true feelings to parents or other adults.

Family dynamics play a role in the development and progression of a teen's depression. During tense or negative conversations with parents, depressed teens become much more emotional than do those without depression. It is often difficult to separate cause from effect—that is, does the family stress cause the depression, or vice versa? Family situations, including parents' marriage problems, teens' difficult relationships with fathers, and high distress in mothers all seem to correlate with increased teen depression. However, some studies show that dysfunctional families are no more likely to have depressed children than healthily functioning families.

DRUG AND ALCOHOL ABUSE

Maybe you've tried making yourself feel better by self-medicating with alcohol or illegal drugs. Almost one-third of people with major depression also abuse alcohol, and teens who have suffered a major depressive episode are twice as likely to start drinking as nondepressed teens.[2] A 1999 study showed that with almost all types of drug abuse, the depression came first. That is, patients began substance abuse to self-medicate their depression. This was

While many teens turn to alcohol and drugs as a means of self-medicating, these harmful substances actually make your depression worse.

particularly true of people addicted to alcohol and cocaine.[3] Scientists think it's likely alcohol abuse and depression share common triggers. They are seeking genes that might be responsible for both conditions.

Self-medication may relieve some symptoms temporarily, but when the alcohol or drug dissipates, the person suffers withdrawal depression, which triggers more alcohol or drug use. Alcohol and drugs can also interfere with the action of antidepressants. It is important to know whether depression or drug abuse came first. A person whose depression came first will need longer-term treatment than one who became depressed due to drug use.

CONDUCT DISORDERS

Conduct disorders include aggressive or physically threatening behavior, destructive behavior such as arson or vandalism, or deceitful behavior such as lying or shoplifting. They may also include violation of rules or age-inappropriate behaviors—for example, running away, skipping school, drinking, or participating in early sexual activity. Depression and other disorders, including anxiety disorder and substance abuse, often co-occur with conduct disorder. Conduct disorders are extremely serious and can result in arrests and other legal problems.

SUICIDAL THOUGHTS AND BEHAVIORS

The longer depression goes untreated, the more hopeless and painful life seems, until sometimes the sufferer looks for a way out. For some, that way out is suicide—the most extreme consequence of untreated depression.

TEEN SUICIDE STATISTICS

- Suicide is the third-leading cause of death among 15- to 24-year-olds. Only homicide and accidents kill more people in this age range.[4]
- Girls are more likely to attempt suicide than boys, but four times as many boys as girls die from suicide.
- Teens with family histories of mental illness, substance abuse, or other suicides are more at risk for suicide.[5]

Fortunately, most depressed people do not kill themselves, but depression does increase the risk of suicide. Teens suffering from substance abuse or aggressive or disruptive behaviors are also at risk. The availability of firearms is a further risk factor—a majority of suicides in youth involve guns.

Although suicide is rare, it is difficult to predict which teens with the risk factors will actually attempt suicide and when. Often, a suicide attempt occurs when a teen, already burdened by depression and possibly another complication, is pushed over the edge by external problems. These external stressors might include disciplinary problems, violence, bullying, or physical or sexual abuse.

Many complications suffer from a sort of chicken and egg problem; that is, it is often difficult to determine which came first. Did a teen turn to drugs because she was depressed, or did she become depressed because she was addicted to drugs? If someone intervenes quickly, treatment can begin and the secondary condition can be prevented. This is the preferred outcome. But complications of depression are separate conditions from the depression itself and must be treated separately. Treating one condition will not make the other one go away, but treating either depression or the complication will help relieve the other condition.

ASK YOURSELF THIS

- *Are you having any complications associated with depression? If so, which ones?*

- *Are external factors deepening your depression? If so, what are they? Can you think of any ways to limit or remove these factors?*

- *What problems, if any, are you having interacting with family or friends? How could you improve these interactions?*

- *Is there at least one family member or other adult you can count on for support?*

4

FINDING OUT WHAT'S WRONG

I t was Madison's first appointment with her new psychiatrist after being diagnosed with depression. She didn't really want to be there, but she didn't have a choice.

Being diagnosed may seem scary and embarrassing, but it's an important first step in handling your depression and recovering.

As she sat down, Dr. Leventhal smiled at her and said, "You look a little nervous. Is anything in particular bothering you?"

"I guess . . . just being here. I feel kind of like a freak, having a mental illness. It's just so embarrassing. My friends are going to think I'm crazy or psycho."

Dr. Leventhal laughed. "Well, you're not crazy or psycho," she said. "Maybe if you understand a little more about what depression is, you'll feel better about it," she said. "Tell me, if you had another illness—say, diabetes—would you be embarrassed?"

Madison considered the question. "No, I guess not," she said. "But that's different. Diabetes is just a normal illness."

Dr. Leventhal raised an eyebrow. "Normal? I'm guessing you mean not brain-related, right?"

Madison nodded.

"You know, the brain is a body organ. Things can go wrong with it, just as they can with the pancreas. When you're depressed, your brain chemicals are out of balance—just like insulin is out of balance in diabetes. Depression is a physical illness. It's not something you caused, and it's not your fault."

"I hadn't thought of it that way," Madison said. "But still, not everyone understands that.

I'm afraid I'll be labeled a nutcase and everyone will laugh at me."

"You can solve that," said Dr. Leventhal, "by being very careful who you tell. Most people don't discuss the details of their medical conditions with just anyone. So, only tell someone if you really want to and if you know that person is a really close friend who you can trust to keep it confidential. They'll support you, and you can teach them about depression and how it's affecting you."

CONFIDE IN SOMEONE

After her first session, Madison still had some doubts, but she felt better. Dr. Leventhal was so positive and had good points. It made her feel therapy might be worthwhile and not something to be embarrassed about. When you first approach a parent or other trusted adult about your depression, you may be very nervous. But once you confide in someone about your depression, that person will help you get the treatment you need. Diagnosis may seem scary, but it's the first step toward feeling better. Remember, as Madison learned, depression is a physical illness. It doesn't get better on its own, but treatment will help you begin enjoying life again. It will also prevent you from spiraling downward into complications such as drug or alcohol abuse.

Putting off help often seems to be the easy way out, but there are many people you can turn to for help in overcoming your fear.

You might want to put off getting help because you fear how people will react to your depression. Talk to your chosen adult about these fears as well. If you are depressed, you might tend to see the worst in a situation, and others can point out the advantages of getting help. They can help you confront your fears. You can also reduce your fears by approaching

WHY TEENS FAIL TO SEEK HELP

Teens have many fears about seeking help for depression. For example, you might have these worries:

- Your friends might think you're crazy or psycho.
- Adults will label you mentally ill.
- You'll have to tell your darkest secrets to a stranger.
- Your parents might learn your darkest secrets.
- Adults might force you to take medication or hospitalize you.

These are all legitimate fears, but they should not keep you from seeking help when you are seriously depressed.

the diagnosis and treatment process in steps. Doing something step by step makes it easier.

THE PROCESS OF DIAGNOSIS

It's time to get help if your symptoms of depression linger for weeks or months. Talk to a parent or someone else you trust, such as a teacher, school counselor, or coach. Sometimes an adult will approach you if he or she has noticed a major change in your behavior. The adult can help you determine a course of action. The process of diagnosis is twofold: first, there should be a visit to the family doctor to rule out other forms of illness, followed by a psychological evaluation conducted by a mental health professional, usually a psychiatrist or psychologist.

The adults helping you will be in charge of finding a competent mental health professional, but you should be involved as much as possible. As the patient, you should trust and feel comfortable with the professional you are seeing. Some mental health counselors are more trained than others. Choose a counselor with a degree in a mental health field and experience working with adolescents. He or she should be licensed by the state or by a professional mental health organization.

PHYSICAL EXAM AND BLOOD TESTS

Some depressive symptoms can be caused by other illnesses, such as illnesses of the central nervous system or endocrine system, the system of glands that release hormones. Some viral diseases can cause symptoms of depression, as can drug use. A medical doctor can rule out these and other illnesses. If you get a clean bill of health, you will undergo a psychological evaluation to make a final diagnosis of depression.

PSYCHOLOGICAL EVALUATION

Psychiatric researchers have classified the symptoms of depression, making them as specific and objective as possible. A psychiatrist diagnoses depression by identifying

If you see a psychiatrist, he or she will try to get you to open up about exactly what is troubling you, what symptoms you have, and how serious the problem is.

the symptoms he or she observes during a psychological evaluation, or clinical interview. This is a structured conversation between the psychiatrist and the teen. The psychiatrist will attempt to assess your situation by asking you questions. In other words, your psychiatrist tries to determine which, if any, of the symptoms on the list for depression you have.

You may be wary of the psychiatrist and feel uncomfortable talking to this stranger about personal problems. You may even worry that the psychiatrist has ulterior motives. These are normal reactions. Remember, though, the psychiatrist's job is to determine the best way to help you, and this is only possible if you answer all questions openly and honestly. He or she has probably talked to many teens, and you're not likely to shock him or her! Your psychiatrist is not there to judge or criticize you—but to be your advocate and help you get through problems you can't handle yourself. This is only possible if you learn to trust your psychiatrist.

PREPARING FOR YOUR APPOINTMENT

During your psychological evaluation, be prepared to answer questions such as:

- **When did people first notice your depression?**
- **How long have you felt depressed?**
- **Does your mood ever change from very depressed to very happy?**
- **Do you ever think about suicide?**
- **Do your symptoms interfere with school, relationships, or activities?**
- **Do you have any close relatives with depression or other mood disorders?**
- **Are you using alcohol, marijuana, or other drugs?**
- **How well do you sleep? Are you sleeping enough or too much?**
- **What, if anything, makes your symptoms better or worse?**
- **How is your diet? Have you recently gained or lost a lot of weight?**

ADJUSTING TO THE DIAGNOSIS

After all tests are completed, you will receive a diagnosis. A depression diagnosis means you meet the criteria in the *DSM-5*. This means you show a depressed mood or a diminished interest or pleasure in activities, or both. You also have four or more of the other symptoms on the list. Your diagnosis will be more specific—you may have major depression, dysthymia, minor depression, bipolar disorder, or cyclothymia, a milder form of bipolar disorder.

Some teens may feel relieved to be diagnosed with depression. It means people are taking their problem seriously and they will get the help they need. These teens are ready to begin their treatment. But others may be shocked or frightened by the diagnosis. They may worry they have been

A NEW FRAMEWORK FOR DIAGNOSIS

The National Institute of Mental Health (NIMH) is developing a new research framework, the Research Domain Criteria (RDoC), for improving the understanding, diagnosis, and treatment of mental health disorders. Instead of relying strictly on identifying symptoms, RDoC will look for objective biological measurements of depression based on genetics and changes in brain function. This could result in precise diagnostic tests comparable to tests for blood pressure or cholesterol. It could also result in new ways to classify mental illnesses.

given a life sentence that will seriously impact, even ruin, their lives. Or they may just not want to be tagged with the stigma of a mental illness. If you feel upset in any way about your diagnosis, it's important to talk with your parent or mental health professional about your concerns. Remember you are not alone. Keep up with friends and activities. Be conscientious about your treatment process, and learn to love yourself.

ASK YOURSELF THIS

- *What concerns do you have about the process of diagnosing your depressive symptoms? How can you overcome these concerns?*

- *Have you confided in a trusted adult and asked for help? If not, why not? How can you overcome your reluctance?*

- *What are the most important things you want the psychological evaluator to know about you?*

- *What questions do you want to ask the psychological evaluator about his or her qualifications?*

- *What concerns do you have about what will happen after your diagnosis?*

5

TREATING DEPRESSION

Zach had been undergoing psychotherapy for his depression, but it didn't seem to be working. By this time, Dr. Evans had expected Zach's mood to improve. But Zach was still very depressed, and he couldn't seem to take an interest in anything. His parents sat in on his session because Dr. Evans wanted to discuss putting Zach on an antidepressant. Both Zach and his parents resisted.

"I don't want to be on drugs," Zach objected. "I don't want to need a drug to be okay."

"The antidepressant will put your brain neurotransmitters back in balance," Dr. Evans said. He continued to explain that Zach's depression was likely to be resistant to psychotherapy alone. "Several people in your family have mood disorders, so there is a genetic connection," he explained. "This type of depression usually requires antidepressants."

His parents worried about safety and the side effects of antidepressants. Zach was already so depressed; they were terrified he would start thinking of suicide.

"But what about the risk of suicide?" his mother asked.

"Suicidal thoughts only occur in a few kids," Dr. Evans said. "But of course, we won't take any chances. We'll monitor Zach closely, and if there's any indication of problems, we'll stop the drug. And Zach, you have to tell your parents immediately if you have any thoughts about hurting yourself."

Finally, Zach and his parents agreed to try the antidepressant. The goal was to lift Zach's depression, and the psychiatrist was the expert, after all.

PSYCHOTHERAPY

The most common types of treatment for depression are psychotherapy and antidepressant medications. Within these two treatments are a variety of possible combinations, which will vary according to your diagnosis, personality type, and the judgment of your therapist. Sometimes, as in Zach's case, the therapist may begin one treatment and change it if the patient does not respond as expected. Changes might involve adding or replacing an antidepressant or changing a dosage.

Typical psychotherapy sessions occur in the therapist's office

FAMILY-FOCUSED THERAPY

Family-focused therapy (FFT) is a type of psychotherapy used primarily to treat bipolar disorder. It includes family members in therapy sessions. Therapists educate the family about the disorder, help identify family conflicts that might be aggravating the illness, and help find ways to resolve the conflicts. They also deal with the stress family members feel when caring for a relative with bipolar disorder. FFT focuses on building communication skills and solving problems as a family.

once a week and last for 30 to 60 minutes.
For teens with mild to moderate depression,
psychotherapy by itself may work well. But
for severe depression, the best option is
often a combination of psychotherapy and
antidepressants. This approach both controls
the current depression and makes it less likely
to recur in the future.

Psychotherapy comes in many forms, which
are tailored to a patient's individual needs. Two
of the most common are cognitive behavioral
therapy (CBT) and interpersonal therapy (IPT).

COGNITIVE BEHAVIORAL THERAPY (CBT)

CBT is a blend of two therapies: cognitive
therapy, which focuses on patients' thoughts and
beliefs, and behavioral therapy, which focuses
on behavior patterns. CBT helps patients
turn negative thought patterns into more
positive thoughts. It also helps them view their
environment and interactions with others more
realistically. It helps them recognize and change
behaviors that might be contributing to their
depression. CBT is very effective for mild or
moderate depression, and it may be combined
with antidepressants.

INTERPERSONAL THERAPY (IPT)

IPT is used to treat depression or dysthymia. It is based on learning and changing communication patterns. Patients learn to identify how they interact with others and to change behaviors and control emotions that are causing problems. Similar to CBT, it may be combined with antidepressants.

ANTIDEPRESSANTS

Antidepressants are medications that alter the function of brain neurotransmitters. Most types affect the neurotransmitters serotonin and norepinephrine; a few affect dopamine. Researchers know these substances improve moods and thus are highly effective in treating depression. However, researchers still know little about how they work.

It takes four to six weeks to see the full effect of antidepressant medication. Also, you must keep taking the medication even when you start to feel better, or depressive symptoms will return. Stopping an antidepressant suddenly can cause withdrawal symptoms. Usually it is stopped gradually, giving the body time to adjust. Antidepressants are not addictive, but people with chronic depression may need to take them indefinitely.

The most commonly used antidepressants are selective serotonin reuptake inhibitors, or

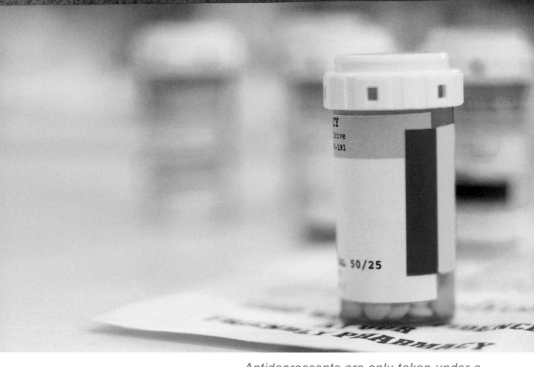

Antidepressants are only taken under a psychiatrist's or other doctor's supervision.

SSRIs. These widely advertised substances include Prozac and Zoloft. SSRIs act on serotonin, a brain neurotransmitter that affects mood. Because serotonin also affects other body functions, such as digestion, pain, sleep, and mental clarity, SSRIs can have many different side effects. Serotonin and norepinephrine reuptake inhibitors (SNRIs), such as Effexor and Cymbalta, form a second group. These are similar to SSRIs, except that they act on two different neurotransmitters: norepinephrine and serotonin. Wellbutrin affects the neurotransmitter dopamine. All three of these groups of antidepressants have side

FDA WARNINGS ABOUT ANTIDEPRESSANTS

Antidepressants, especially SSRIs, are effective in treating depression, but they may have unintended side effects. A 2004 Food and Drug Administration (FDA) study showed that 4 percent of children and adolescents taking antidepressants considered or attempted suicide, compared to only 2 percent of those taking a placebo. In 2005, the FDA adopted a "black-box" label (its most serious warning) for all antidepressants, emphasizing the need to monitor children and adolescents for suicidal thoughts and behavior. In 2007, they extended the warning to include young adults through age 24.[1]

effects, but the side effects are not usually serious.

COMBINING MEDICATION AND PSYCHOTHERAPY

Treatment regimens for adolescents are based on data from studies of depressed adults and a few studies on depressed adolescents. But because there are few studies on adolescents, many treatment regimens are also based on trial and error by psychiatrists conducting the treatment. Teens with mild or moderate depression usually receive psychotherapy alone. If there is no improvement within six to 12 weeks, the psychiatrist may add an antidepressant. Teens with severe depression usually receive a combination of psychotherapy and antidepressants from the beginning.

Studies funded by the NIMH have verified that a combination of psychotherapy and antidepressants are the most effective treatments for depressed teens. Studies include the Treatment for Adolescents with Depression Study (TADS) and the Treatment of SSRI-Resistant Depression in Adolescents (TORDIA) study. The TORDIA study found that teens who do not respond when first treated with antidepressants will improve if they are switched to a treatment including psychotherapy as well as medication. Also, the Treatment of Adolescent Suicide Attempters (TASA) study showed greatest success occurred with medication plus a specialized type of psychotherapy designed to reduce suicidal thinking and behavior. But when teens also suffer from a coexisting disorder, such as

BRAIN STIMULATION THERAPIES

When depression is resistant to typical treatments, some patients may choose to try a form of electrical stimulation called electroconvulsive therapy (ECT). ECT sends small amounts of electric current through both sides of the brain, altering the function of the brain's neurotransmitters. The patient is given an anesthetic and a muscle relaxant to sleep through the treatment. The treatment takes 10 to 15 minutes, after which the patient is awake and alert. The patient receives treatments several times weekly for several weeks. Side effects may include confusion and memory loss, but usually these are short-term. ECT once had a bad reputation, but technologies have greatly improved, and ECT can help in cases where other treatments have not worked.

HOSPITALIZATION FOR DEPRESSION

Teens who are severely depressed and at risk for suicide may be hospitalized for a short time so specialists can monitor them closely and bring their symptoms under control. During this time, a treatment team including a psychiatrist, psychologist, social worker, or others trained in psychiatric care will interact with these teens. They may receive antidepressant medication and have individual, group, or family therapy sessions. They may also do other activities including exercise, schoolwork, or art or music therapy.

substance abuse, they are less likely to respond to treatments for depression.[2] Studies on adolescent depression are focusing on risk factors and ways of pinpointing the condition so early intervention and effective treatment are possible.

ASK YOURSELF THIS

- *How do you feel about undergoing psychotherapy? Do you think talking about your depression will help you control it?*

- *Which type of psychotherapy, CBT or IPT, do you think you would prefer? Why?*

- *How do you feel about taking antidepressants? Are you concerned about your safety? How could you stay safe when taking antidepressants?*

- *Do you think any other types of therapies would be useful to you? Which ones? Why?*

- *What future advances in adolescent depression treatment would you most like to see? Why?*

LIFESTYLE CHANGES AND ALTERNATIVE TREATMENTS

S ofia was having a bad day. She had started to control her depression, but today all the negative thoughts had come back. School was hard, relationships were hard, and she was so tired. She sighed heavily.

Talk to a trusted friend. Perhaps he or she has helpful advice in dealing with your thoughts and feelings.

"Bad thoughts getting you down again?" asked her best friend, Mellie. They were sitting together outside, unwinding after school.

"Yeah," said Sofia. Mellie was the only friend who knew about her depression, and she was grateful for Mellie's support.

"You know," Mellie said. "I have an idea. I know you think I'm flaky sometimes, but I know something that might help—I know it helps me."

"You don't need help," Sofia said. "You're always in a good mood. But I'll bite. What might help?"

Mellie looked a little nervous. "Guided imagery. And maybe I'm always in a good mood because of it."

Sofia was intrigued in spite of herself. "What's guided imagery?"

"Let's go to my house and try it."

They leaned back on comfortable chairs on Mellie's deck. They closed their eyes. Mellie described being in a hot-air balloon, up where it was really quiet. You looked down and saw the world below, but you were away from all the stresses. You let all your bad thoughts drop over the edge and away.

As Mellie talked, Sofia felt more and more relaxed and peaceful. Her depressing thoughts and worries melted away.

Finally, Mellie brought the hot-air balloon down to a soft landing in a secret place that only they knew about. Sofia opened her eyes slowly and looked at her friend. "That was amazing," she said. "Can we do that again?"

Mellie laughed. "We can do it whenever you'd like."

WHAT CAN YOU DO?

Many teens with depression think, "I should be able to take it" or "I'll get over it eventually." But depression is a medical condition that requires treatment. You must take your medications exactly as prescribed and go to your appointments faithfully to get better. There are also many things you can do in your everyday life to lessen your depression.

STAYING HEALTHY

Everyone should live a healthy lifestyle, but it is particularly important if you are depressed. One of the best ways to lift your mood is exercise. Activity keeps your body healthy and also boosts your production of happy brain chemicals such as serotonin and endorphins. In one study, patients who walked or cycled 30 to 40 minutes per day for four days per week showed a decrease in depression symptoms that lasted for

Exercise is beneficial for both your physical and mental health. Take some time to ride your bike or go for a walk.

a year after the study. Similar results occurred with resistance training.[1]

Good nutrition and sleep are important, too. Eating small, well-balanced meals throughout the day will decrease mood swings. Avoid sugary foods—they will give you a quick high, but a sugar crash will follow quickly. Complex carbohydrates such as whole grains provide the same energy but are broken down more slowly. Lack of sleep makes you irritable and depressed as well as tired. Seven to nine hours of sleep per night keeps most people well rested.

BUILDING RESILIENCE

The APA lists ten ways to build resilience:

- **Connect with family and friends; accept their help and support.**
- **Don't let crises overwhelm you; change how you respond to events.**
- **Accept change as part of life.**
- **Develop and move toward small, realistic goals.**
- **Take decisive action; don't expect problems to go away.**
- **Learn about yourself.**
- **Develop a positive view of yourself.**
- **Keep things in perspective.**
- **Cultivate a hopeful, optimistic outlook.**
- **Take care of your health, needs, and feelings.[2]**

Also, being isolated deepens depression, so doing things with friends and family is essential. Keep those who love you in your life, even when you don't really feel like it. Joining a group or volunteering for a worthy cause can also raise your mood. Finally, learn to be resilient. Resilience is the ability to adapt well to stress and changes in your life and to bounce back from adversity. Remind yourself to go with the flow instead of sinking into depression.

COMPLEMENTARY AND ALTERNATIVE MEDICINE

Complementary and alternative medicine (CAM) consists of natural health treatments not accepted as standard practice. Most Western medical practitioners are not convinced these treatments are effective for moderate or severe depression. However, people who prefer natural treatments may use CAM methods as supplements to standard treatments with their doctor's permission. Most CAM therapies can be classified as either herbal supplements and remedies or as relaxation techniques.

HERBAL REMEDIES AND SUPPLEMENTS

Supplements are vitamins, minerals, or other chemicals required for good nutrition. They are taken in pill form to ensure sufficient dietary nutrients. Deficiencies in omega-3 fatty acids, magnesium, and B vitamins (B_1, folic acid, B_6, and B_{12}) are known to increase depression. Vitamin D deficiency

SAINT-JOHN'S-WORT

In Europe, the herbal remedy Saint-John's-wort is used routinely to treat mild and moderate depression. But in the United States, it is considered an alternative remedy, and medical practitioners do not prescribe it. A US study showed Saint-John's-wort was no more effective than a placebo (sugar pill) in treating symptoms of severe depression.[3] However, several German and British studies showed it was just as effective as antidepressants and had fewer side effects.[4] Before using Saint-John's-wort as an alternative treatment, you should consult a doctor.

is associated with SAD. These substances are all available as supplements. Herbal remedies are medications. The best-known herbal remedy used to treat depression is Saint-John's-wort (*Hypericum perforatum*). Studies in Europe and elsewhere have shown its effectiveness, but it must be used with your doctor's permission because it interacts with some prescribed drugs.

RELAXATION TECHNIQUES

Relaxation techniques help control depression, but their effect is less than that of psychological treatments, such as CBT. However, doctors may recommend relaxation techniques to supplement your medical treatment. These techniques reduce stress and improve your feelings of well-being. Typical relaxation techniques include deep breathing, progressive muscle relaxation, meditation, yoga, and guided imagery.

Deep breathing is slow and completely fills and empties your lungs. It calms the mind and relaxes the body. Progressive muscle relaxation involves contracting and then relaxing the muscles of each body region: face and head first, followed by neck and shoulders, hands and arms, abdomen, and legs and feet. Many athletes and musicians use these techniques to prepare themselves before games or concerts.

Meditation is an altered state of consciousness that promotes relaxation and can help control depression. Meditation requires a comfortable, quiet place. You must relax your breathing and focus your attention. In transcendental meditation, you focus on a mantra, a word or phrase that calms you, and repeat it silently to yourself, trying to achieve stillness and eliminate distracting thoughts. In meditation, you try to be very aware of the present moment. You let thoughts and emotions flow through you, trying not to respond to them.

Hatha yoga, the most common form of yoga in the United States, combines physical poses with controlled breathing, followed by a short period of relaxation or meditation. It relaxes the body by reducing heart rate, blood pressure, and respiration. This reduces stress and improves mood. Limited studies have shown yoga is effective in treating depression, but more research needs to be done.

Guided imagery, or visualization, is a form of meditation in which you choose a mental

PET THERAPY

According to psychiatrist Dr. Ian Cook, "Pets offer an unconditional love that can be very helpful to people with depression."[5] Pets can help relieve depression by providing uncomplicated love, social interaction, companionship, and touch. They also help the person with depression establish a routine and responsibility.

Man's best friend and other pets can help in your recovery.

image that relaxes you, such as the hot-air balloon Mellie and Sofia used. You use all your senses to visualize your image and relax as completely as possible. You may do this in your mind, write out your image, or make a tape of yourself describing it and play it back during each session. This process reduces stress and makes it easier to let go of anxious and depressing thoughts.

In short, while medical intervention is necessary, you can also be an active participant in your recovery from depression. You can develop and maintain a healthy lifestyle, and with the help of your doctor or therapist you can find alternative treatments to help you relax and feel better.

ASK YOURSELF THIS

- *Do you currently have a healthy lifestyle? What aspects could you improve? How?*

- *Do you think dietary supplements or herbal remedies would help your depression? Why or why not?*

- *Have you ever tried guided imagery as Mellie did to help with your feelings of depression?*

- *Which relaxation techniques would you like to learn and use? Why did you pick these?*

- *How do you think relaxation techniques might help ease your depression?*

KEEPING PEOPLE IN YOUR LIFE

Tamara had just received a text from Lily. She and Amira were going to a movie and they wanted Tamara to go. Six months ago, she would have jumped at the chance. But now, she felt really sad and tired. She just

wanted to stay in her room and pull the covers
over her head.

She rolled over in bed and texted back, "No,
sorry, busy." That should take care of it, she
thought. But she underestimated her friends.

Lily showed Tamara's text to Amira. They
looked at each other.

"That's it!" said Amira. "It's time to do
something."

Lily and Amira had watched for the last few
months as Tamara pulled away more and more.
They talked about it a lot, wondering why she
kept refusing to get together. There didn't seem
to be a reason. They hadn't had a fight and
things were going well. Sure, high school was
tough and they were really busy, but they had
always found time for fun. Until recently.

The girls went to Tamara's house. "Can
we talk?" Lily asked Tamara's mother. They
sat in the kitchen and discussed the situation.
Tamara's mother was worried, too. She hadn't
told her yet, but she had made an appointment
for Tamara to see a psychologist next week.

"But right now," she said, "let's see if we can
get her to go out with you. She needs to get out
of the house and do something."

The three of them confronted Tamara
in her room. Her mother told her about the

appointment. Amira said, "No excuses! You're coming with us. It will do you good to get out and see people."

Tamara watched Lily go through her closet and find her an outfit. She sighed. But deep down, she felt relief. She was glad they cared enough to help her.

DEPRESSION CAN SABOTAGE RELATIONSHIPS

Teenagers often sleep a lot. Rapid growth and hormone changes sometimes mess with your normal day-night cycles. A teen who has been running all week trying to fit in school, homework, activities, and friends may be exhausted by the weekend. But when you start avoiding friends, take no pleasure in things you used to enjoy, and only want to sleep, something is wrong, and—as in Tamara's case—friends and family begin to notice.

Depression can take a toll on teens' relationships when they need them most. During the teen years, kids learn to develop and maintain relationships with family members, friends, and peers. Depression hinders that social development and compounds normal teenage feelings of self-doubt and inadequacy. This can be a particular problem for teens with quiet, shy temperaments who don't make friends

If you don't have close trusted friends to turn to, talk with your family members. They will always be there for you and want to help.

easily. They may already feel isolated, and when depression hits, they may lack a social network to support them through the worst times.

Teens whose depression occurs with or because of other problems in their lives may find relationships even more difficult to sustain. Teens who are rebellious, sullen, dishonest, or overly impulsive often push away both adults and peers. But without help, these behaviors may progress to conduct disorders and even police involvement. Teens struggling with sexual identity are a very different group, but they are also at great risk. LGBT teens may be bullied, humiliated, and socially isolated by their peers. In the worst cases, even parents may reject them.

Whether or not your depression is compounded by other difficulties, it is vital you develop and sustain relationships. Ideally, relationships with family and friends should be paramount. But support groups, both local and online, can be lifelines for you if you are missing the support of family and friends.

THE IMPORTANCE OF FAMILY AND FRIENDS

For most teens, a loving family is the starting point for managing depression. Even if you have withdrawn from family members and don't feel comfortable discussing your feelings, try to do it anyway. These are the people who will always be there. You can ask them for help and support. Sometimes you know you are depressed, but your parents may think you're just acting up. Learn to recognize patterns in your symptoms, perhaps by keeping a journal of your thoughts and feelings. Point out these patterns when you talk to a parent, explain how you feel, and ask for help.

Spending time with friends and doing things you love or used to love is also essential to overcoming depression. When you are depressed, you often want to retreat into your shell, as Tamara did, and avoid friends and activities. It is important you make yourself spend time with close friends and participate in social activities. These simple acts will decrease your depression.

You might be concerned about sharing your feelings even with close friends. You might be afraid they will judge you or no longer want to be your friends. A good friend will be concerned and want to help. Think of how you would feel if your best friend was going through the same thing. Overcome your feelings of discomfort and talk to your close friends. Explain what is happening with you and ask for their support. You might be surprised at the positive response.

INVOLVING FAMILIES

Because depression affects the entire family, some psychiatrists involve the family in diagnosis. Dr. Nassir Ghaemi, professor of psychiatry and pharmacology at Tufts Medical Center in Boston, Massachusetts, says this is especially important for diagnosing bipolar disorder. Half of patients do not recognize when they are having a manic episode; family members are twice as likely to recognize these behaviors. In addition, Dr. Ghaemi says once treatment is underway, it is important for parents to remind the depressed patient to stay on his or her medication.[1]

FINDING SUPPORT GROUPS LOCALLY AND ONLINE

Sometimes you may need more support than family or friends can provide. Or, it might be easier to talk to a stranger than to someone close. Local or regional depression support groups can help in these situations. Some support groups are run by medical professionals, such as psychiatrists, psychologists, or social workers; others may be self-help groups in which people with depression come together regularly to talk and help each other.

You can find out about support groups from your doctor or therapist or by searching online. Web sites vary, but many contain discussion and chat groups, forums where you can ask and answer questions,

EXPLAINING YOUR DEPRESSION TO OTHERS

When starting a conversation about your problems, be as honest and straightforward as possible. Say something such as, "I'm feeling really down and nothing seems to matter anymore. I think I'm depressed. Will you help me?" Or, "I'm doing drugs and I need to stop. What can I do?" Or, "I'm afraid of the thoughts I'm having. I've been thinking a lot about death and dying. I need someone to help me." If it is too difficult to discuss these things in person, try putting your feelings in a letter, story, or poem, and give it to your parent or friend.

Be proactive about your depression recovery. If you're not comfortable speaking to someone about your depression, know that you can find some helpful resources online.

informative articles, and lists of resources. Some are specifically oriented toward teenagers.

If you are in a crisis situation—for example, if you are extremely depressed and considering suicide or are in an abusive family situation—crisis centers and crisis hotlines can give you immediate help. A crisis center is staffed by trained professionals and provides counseling and care to individuals and families. A crisis

hotline is a telephone number you can call
24 hours a day to talk about your problems. It is
staffed by mental health professionals or trained
volunteers. You can find crisis centers and
hotlines online or in the Yellow Pages.

HELPING YOURSELF THROUGH DEPRESSION

The help of other people is essential as you
work through your depression, but in the end,
you are responsible for your own recovery.
You must do the hard work. You must diligently
follow the steps in your treatment program—go
to psychotherapy sessions, do your homework,
and take your medication. Learn about
depression. Understand that it is treatable
and that, with the help of family, friends, and
professionals, you can overcome it.

ONLINE SUPPORT GROUPS

These organizations (and others) have online support
groups:

- Anxiety and Depression Association of America (ADAA):
  http://www.adaa.org/finding-help/getting-support
- Depression and Bipolar Support Alliance
  (DBSA): http://www.dbsalliance.org/site/
  PageServer?pagename=peer_support_group_locator
- National Alliance on Mental Illness (NAMI): http://
  www.nami.org/Template.cfm?section=Find_Support
- Psych Central: http://psychcentral.com/
  resources/Depression/Support_Groups

ASK YOURSELF THIS

- *Have any of your friends or family members mentioned your depression? If so, how did you respond?*

- *Have you discussed your depression with a parent or sibling? If so, how did they respond?*

- *Do you feel comfortable confiding your depression to close friends? What would make you more comfortable doing this?*

- *Have you tried to relieve your depression by doing activities? If so, how did this change your mood?*

- *Have you ever used a support group? If so, was it helpful? In what way?*

TIPS FOR SURVIVING DEPRESSION

Bev Cobain, RN, has developed seven tips to help teens survive depression:

- "Get Some Exercise." Releasing endorphins produces a natural high.
- "Take a Break." Rest and relax when you need to.
- "Have Some Fun." Laugh and be social.
- "Eat Good Food." Eat more fruits and veggies, less fat and sugar.
- "Talk about It." Don't bottle up feelings.
- "Stick with It." Commit to your treatment plan.
- "Feed Your Spirit." Do things that make you feel better.[2]

8

HELPING A DEPRESSED TEEN

L ayla was in charge of decorations for the Fall Dance. She was amazed when David turned down her request for help. David was an artist, and he usually loved doing anything creative. But lately, he had been acting weird.

Deciphering a friend's feelings and actions can be difficult. If you notice one of your friends acting depressed, it's important to know how to help.

For the first month of school, he seemed really hyper. He laughed and joked all the time and bragged about being the world's greatest artist. Now, it was like someone had flipped his switch. When Layla talked to him, he seemed very down. He barely looked at her and showed no interest in working on the decorations. Both behaviors—bragging and lack of interest—were unlike him.

"David, what's wrong?" she asked. "Did something happen? Why are you so depressed?"

"Nothing. I'm fine," he said. "Gotta go." And he left.

Layla was sure she hadn't done anything to hurt David's feelings. That night, she called and asked why he didn't want to work on the decorations. He was silent for a moment and then said, "I just don't feel like it. I'm not that good anyway. You can find someone better."

"Who?" Layla demanded. "There is no one better. You know that—just last week you were bragging about being the best."

"Yeah, well, I was being an idiot." He sounded embarrassed. "I know I'm really a loser. You guys would be better off without me."

"Whoa! That's pretty intense," Layla said. "What do you mean by that, exactly?"

"Oh, nothing," David said, and hung up.

Layla was shaken by the phone call. David almost sounded suicidal. She talked to her mother, who said it sounded as if David needed help. They decided that first thing tomorrow morning, Layla would see the school counselor and ask him to help David.

HELPING A FAMILY MEMBER

Usually, a family member or close friend is first to notice when a teen is depressed. Even if you aren't familiar with the symptoms of depression, you can often tell if someone is behaving differently from normal, such as David's changes in personality. Sometimes someone may just be having a bad day, but if the behavior persists, it might be serious. If you think a family member, such as a parent, may be depressed but aren't sure, take action. It's always better to be safe than sorry. The question is, what should you do? If you are concerned about the behavior of someone in your family, first make sure you recognize the symptoms of depression. A depressed parent may show signs of sadness, sleep more often, and lose interest in activities they used to enjoy. Also, realize you cannot fix the depressed person. Don't expect your family member to just snap out of it. Ultimately, that person is responsible for his or her own recovery.

One of the most important things you can do is offer your unconditional support. They may feel ashamed, embarrassed, or afraid of being misunderstood. It will be hard for them to talk about their feelings. Let them know you are available to listen, but don't pressure them. Family members may insist that nothing is wrong, but trust your instincts. They may not realize they are depressed or may be in denial.

HOW TO TALK TO A DEPRESSED FRIEND OR FAMILY MEMBER

Emphasize your willingness to listen, even when the teen doesn't want to talk, but don't pressure. You might start a conversation by saying, "I've been concerned about you lately; you seem depressed." When he or she is ready to talk, listen without judgment. Don't lecture or offer advice unless asked. Don't try to talk the person out of depression. Emphasize that he or she is not alone, and ask what you can do right now to help. Recognize that the person might need many conversations to process his or her feelings.

Finally, suggest the possibility of counseling or professional help, explaining that depression is a medical illness and not a reason for shame. If the depression is severe or your family member seems suicidal, don't wait. Never ignore talk of suicide. Contact a doctor or emergency medical personnel immediately. When the person is in treatment, continue your support by making sure he or she goes to therapy sessions and takes medications on schedule.

HELPING A FRIEND

A friend can do many of the same things as a parent or family member. Be aware of depressive symptoms and recognize when something is wrong. Let your friend know you support him or her and are willing to talk at any time. If your friend won't talk, but you're worried, talk with his or her parents or another adult, such as a school counselor. Tell them what behaviors you have seen and why you are worried. Let them know you think your friend needs help.

Make sure your friend is included in gatherings of family and friends. Invite him or her specifically and offer to drive. A depressed friend may not automatically assume he or she

THINGS NOT TO SAY TO A DEPRESSED PERSON

Sometimes what we don't say is as important as what we do say. Here are some statements that do *not* help a depressed person and you should never say:

- "Just snap out of it!"
- "You're no fun to be around."
- "You know what your problem is . . ."
- "You wouldn't be depressed if you'd just . . ."
- "You're just being lazy," or "You're just faking it."

Keep your depressed friend involved. Propose a movie or shopping so he or she feels accepted and included.

is invited and may even resist going. Offer to help with everyday things, such as shopping or doing laundry. Sometimes just doing a chore with another person makes it easier. Also, do fun things together—go to lunch or a movie, play a video game, take a walk, or visit the beach. Spending time with and involving the person in activities lets your friend know you care and can help lift the depression.

WHEN SUICIDE THREATENS

Although most depression responds well to psychotherapy and antidepressants, a depressed person is not thinking clearly and rationally, and sometimes, suicide may seem to be their only choice. Friends, family, and caregivers should always be alert for the warning signs of suicide and be ready to take immediate action to prevent it.

Talk to your friend about his or her thoughts and feelings. Ask if they are thinking of suicide, or if they have a suicide plan. If they have a plan, they are more likely to attempt suicide. Try to keep your friend safe. Let his or her parents know if your friend has anything that may be used to commit suicide, such as a gun or pills. Contact your friend's parents and describe the situation. In some cases, adjusting or changing medications may help eliminate suicidal thoughts.

SUICIDE WARNING SIGNS

A teen may be at risk of suicide if he or she:

- Talks about suicide, death, or dying ("I wish I were dead," "You'd be better off without me.")
- Says good-bye to people or gives away belongings
- Obtains the means to commit suicide, such as stockpiling pills or buying a gun
- Does risky or self-destructive things
- Withdraws from friends and wants to be left alone
- Shows feelings of self-hate or of being trapped or hopeless
- Changes normal routine
- Has major mood swings

If your friend is threatening suicide or is in a crisis situation, call a suicide hotline number immediately. You can call 911 or the National Suicide Prevention Lifeline (1-800-873-273-TALK). Or locate community resources you can contact for help.

ASK YOURSELF THIS

- *Do you know the signs of depression and suicide? Can you recognize them in another person?*

- *Do you have a friend who seems depressed? What signs of depression do you see?*

- *In what ways can you support your depressed friend or family member?*

- *What can you do if you think your friend or family member is having suicidal thoughts?*

WHERE TO GO FOR HELP

If you're concerned a friend or family member is depressed, there are many professional resources you can turn to for help. Visit or contact your local or state clinics, hospital psychiatry departments, community mental health centers, or family services. Perhaps there's a mental health specialist, such as a psychologist or psychiatrist, you can speak with about your friend or family member.

9

YOUR FUTURE WITH DEPRESSION

A t his last psychotherapy session, Emilio had confessed his fears about the future. Now a senior in high school, he had been diagnosed with severe depression as a freshman and had been on medication since then. Although his depression was under control and psychotherapy had helped a lot, he was worried about college and beyond.

"How will I function away from home?" he wondered. "Here, I've got my parents to help. They make sure I take my medication, and they notice if I'm starting to go downhill. And I've got you."

"It's normal to be worried," Dr. Fenton assured Emilio. "College will be a big adjustment, and you need to be prepared. Let's think about what we can do to make sure you have a smooth transition."

Together, Emilio and Dr. Fenton came up with ways Emilio could prepare. Dr. Fenton offered to discuss Emilio's situation with someone at the university health center and to locate a new psychiatrist. He suggested Emilio have one or both parents check in with him every day by phone or video chat. He urged Emilio to remember to take his medication and to ask for help when he needed it. And he assured Emilio he was always available by phone.

"The best way to avoid recurrence of your depression is to stay on top of it," he explained. "It won't go away, but you can control it."

"I guess you're right, but I keep thinking about the rest of my life and how much trouble this disease is," Emilio admitted. "Won't there ever be a cure?"

"Probably not a cure," Dr. Fenton admitted. "But treatments are improving, so don't give up hope! If you want, we can spend part of your next session talking about possible new treatments."

"I'd like that," Emilio said. "It will give me something to look forward to."

MANAGING DEPRESSION

There is no absolute cure for depression—you can't take an antibiotic as you can for a bacterial infection. But that doesn't mean there's no hope. Depression is very treatable, and treatment is successful for most people. But depression is considered a chronic illness. Under certain conditions, it can recur, and if it does you must be treated again.

It is difficult to develop effective new treatments because researchers are still learning how the brain works and how it changes during depression. Also, the causes of depression are complex and vary from one individual to another. Treatments that work for one person may not work for you. Finally, there are few studies documenting how well different treatments work for adolescents. Doctors and researchers are working hard to develop new and improved treatments for depression. Some are modifications of existing treatments or new ways of delivering treatment. Others are entirely new.

One difficulty in treating depression is that many people do not get the help they need. A 2003 survey indicated that only half of those suffering from depression in the past 12 months had received treatment and only 18 to 25 percent received adequate treatment.[1] Sometimes teens refuse to consider treatment or are uncomfortable talking face-to-face to a stranger about personal problems. Maybe you lack convenient access to psychotherapists or cannot afford psychotherapy. One potential solution to these problems is Internet-based self-help therapy.

LONG-TERM MANAGEMENT OF DEPRESSION

Chronic depression can be diagnosed and managed with ongoing intervention by a family doctor. In a recent study, doctors, nurses, and office staff were taught to provide simple care, including assessments of depression symptoms, telephone calls, and information on treatment options. The goal was to encourage depressed patients to seek and continue treatment. Depressed patients increased use of both antidepressants and psychotherapy during the two-year study, and their depressive symptoms decreased 33 percent more than the nonintervention group.[2]

*With the Internet at our fingertips,
it is becoming easier to take part in
Internet-based therapy, such as ICBT.*

INTERNET-DELIVERED COGNITIVE BEHAVIORAL THERAPY (ICBT)

ICBT has been found to be effective, especially when delivered in a structured format, such as guided self-help, in which the patient follows a manual and receives therapist contact by e-mail. Some researchers are also designing Internet-based interventions to supplement depression treatment rather than replace it.

Internet treatment of depression is one aspect of the new field of telemedicine, or delivery of mental health care by satellite, Internet, telephone, and other remote methods.

In addition, team-based diagnosis, which involves several specialists, and follow-up care provided by primary medical practices (your family doctor), rather than specialized mental health centers that treat only mental health patients, should make mental health care more available for teens in the future.

NEW DRUGS FOR DEPRESSION

Scientists' limited understanding of the biological causes of depression makes it difficult to develop new antidepressants. But new research suggests that the definition of depression is much broader than previously thought. It is a chronic illness that affects and is affected by not only the brain and nervous system but also the endocrine (hormone) system and the body's biological rhythms, such as sleep-wake cycles. Researchers are considering various additional neurotransmitters as targets for future drugs. In addition, levels of stress hormones, such as cortisol, affect moods, so tweaking the endocrine system may lead to new drugs.

Most promising is a potential new generation of fast-acting antidepressants. One problem with current antidepressants is the long delay. It can take two to six weeks or more before the patient feels the effects. A new drug, GLYX-13, shows relief within hours

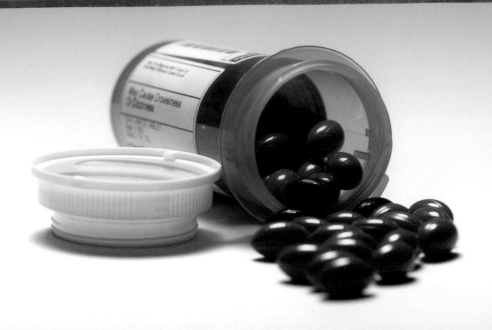

Researchers are always working on antidepressant improvements, including faster-acting antidepressants.

for previously medication-resistant patients. The drug appears to be safe, with only mild to moderate side effects, and the effects of one dose last approximately seven days. GLYX-13 targets brain receptors involved in learning and memory. It may also be effective in treating bipolar disorder and anxiety.

NEW OR IMPROVED TECHNOLOGIES

New technologies in depression research target brain and genetic functions. In a study from King's College London, scientists used blood-flow patterns in the brain to correctly

predict responses of 80 percent of patients to
CBT. Using Magnetic Resonance Imaging (MRI)
scans of brain structure, they correctly predicted
nearly 90 percent of responders. These results
provide strong evidence that depression is
associated with specific brain changes.[3] If
scientists can devise quick tests to measure
these biological markers, they can target future
depression treatments much more precisely.

Scientists are also trying to identify gene
targets that can help us understand biological
causes of depression. However, genes identified
with mental illness have crossover effects.
For example, the same genes associated with
bipolar disorder are also associated with the
mental disorders schizophrenia and autism.
Understanding these connections could lead to
new ways of classifying mental disorders.

There is also progress in predicting
responses to medication based on genes.
Several studies have scanned human genomes
looking for tiny variations from normal that
might predict responses to medication. Although
variations in single genes within a person's
genome are not good predictors of medication
responses, researchers hope that variations
in groups of genes may be better. Finally,
advancements in electroconvulsive therapy
(ECT) have helped control depression while

decreasing the memory loss that was once a side effect.

Although progress in understanding brain function has been slow to develop, researchers are now poised for breakthroughs in several areas. Now, doctors often must try two or three different types of medications or psychotherapies before finding the right one. The key to any new treatment for depression will be developing more personalized treatments that take into account differences in each patient's metabolism and brain function. Today's research is geared toward methods for predicting individual responses to a given therapy so each patient receives treatment that best fits his or her needs.

In the meantime, many caring medical professionals, parents, and friends are already providing excellent care based on the best information currently

DEEP BRAIN STIMULATION

A new technique of deep brain stimulation can measure levels of brain neurotransmitters in real time. The technology, called Wireless Instantaneous Neurotransmitter Concentration System (WINCS), measures serotonin, dopamine, and norepinephrine—all correlated with depression. Researchers hope this ability to measure neurotransmitters so precisely will soon lead to methods for controlling their levels and improving treatment of depression.

available. If you are a teen who hasn't yet reached out for help with your depression, it's time you did!

ASK YOURSELF THIS

- *Are you worried about how you will deal with your depression once you finish high school? What worries you most?*

- *What plans have you made for how you will deal with your depression after high school?*

- *What problems, if any, have you had with your depression treatments so far? What improvements would you like to see?*

- *Would you consider telemedicine, such as ICBT, for treating your depression? Why or why not?*

- *Of the new advances listed, which ones do you think show the most promise?*

JUST THE FACTS

Classifications of depression include major depression (severe enough to be disabling), dysthymia (less severe but longer lasting), minor depression (less severe but may develop into major depression), and bipolar disorder, which presents alternating manic and depressive states.

The average age of onset of depression in teens is 15, but it is common in those aged 10–14. Girls are twice as likely as boys to suffer from depression.

Depression is a biologically based disease with a genetic component, meaning it runs in families. It results from imbalances in brain neurotransmitters and sometimes hormones.

Environmental stressors can also trigger depression, especially in those already biologically prone to it. These include bullying, childhood traumas such as abuse, and other forms of severe stress.

Suicide is the most serious consequence of depression. It is the third-leading cause of death among 15- to 24-year-olds. Only homicides and accidents kill more youth.

Bullying is a major risk factor for development of depression in teens. Those most likely to be bullied are members of groups seen as different, including LGBT teens, the disabled, and those belonging to a race, ethnicity, or religion different from the majority.

Depression is diagnosed by a psychological evaluation (clinical interview) with a psychiatrist or similar professional. Besides sadness and/or diminished interest or pleasure in activities, a depressed person shows at least four other signs and symptoms involving sleep, appetite, activity levels, feelings of guilt or worthlessness, problems with thinking or concentration, or thoughts of death.

The major forms of treatment for depression are psychotherapy (often cognitive behavioral therapy) and antidepressant medications. Mild or moderate depression is often treated with psychotherapy alone. Severe, or biologically based, depression nearly always requires use of antidepressants. Often, a combination of antidepressants and psychotherapy works best.

A teen with depression can improve his or her condition by maintaining a healthy lifestyle, building resilience to life changes, and developing relaxation techniques to relieve stress and defuse negative thoughts. Being active and staying connected to friends and relatives are also important.

There is no absolute cure for depression. Treatment is usually successful, but depression episodes may recur throughout life.

WHERE TO TURN

If You Need Help with Depression

If you have been feeling sad, depressed, or angry for more than two weeks, and if you have lost interest in being around friends or doing activities you used to enjoy, you may be suffering from depression. Ask a trusted adult—such as a parent, teacher, or counselor—for help. Explain how you are feeling and how the depression is affecting your life. An adult can locate an appropriate mental health professional who can test you for depression and either provide treatment or refer you to a treatment center. Do not wait for depression to subside; it is a physical illness and needs to be treated. Even though asking for help may be frightening, it is necessary for you to get better.

If You Feel Alone with Your Depression

Depression can be a very lonely illness. Many teens feel embarrassed about having a mental illness and worry how others will react. There is no need to tell everyone, but it is important to have a support group. Confide in one or two close friends who will support you and keep your situation confidential. Explain what depression is, how it is affecting you, and what your treatment involves. Ask for their support and explain how they can help you. If you don't feel comfortable confiding in friends, try an online depression support group, such as those found at Teen Moods at www.teen-moods.net and Teen Depression Community at www.medhelp.org/forums/Teen-Depression/show/185

If You Are Being Bullied or Harassed

Some teens seem to take pleasure in bullying or harassing those who are different from them. Bullies have problems themselves, but that's small comfort if you're on the receiving end of their hateful actions. Bullying is not always physical. A bully might beat you up or steal your belongings, but he or she may also say mean, vicious things about you. Bullied teens often suffer in silence, afraid things will get worse if they tell someone, or they're too humiliated to ask for help. But no one deserves this kind of treatment, and it needs to be stopped immediately. You can do this by telling an adult—a parent, teacher, or school counselor—what's going on. Do this at once. You have a right to feel safe and to be treated with respect.

If You Are Thinking about Suicide

If you are having thoughts such as, "I'd be better off dead," or "There's nothing to live for anymore," you need to get help immediately. Even though you may feel extremely hopeless, this is the depression talking, and you need to be with someone who is objective and realistic—someone who can remind you of all the reasons for living. If you are having suicidal thoughts, immediately go to a parent or trusted friend and tell them. Ask them to help you. They can talk you through it and can take you to an emergency room or a mental health professional. You can also call for help yourself. Call 911 or the National Suicide Prevention Lifeline at 1-800-273-8255 (1-800-273 TALK).

If a Peer You Know Is Depressed or Suicidal

Get help for a depressed peer as soon as possible. If you wait, his or her depression will deepen and become harder to treat. Talk with your peer and get him or her to open up about the depression. But also find professional help. If you are a friend, tell your friend's parents or another adult who can get help. If your friend is suicidal, or if you think he or she may be, act immediately! Take your friend to an emergency room or to his or her psychiatrist or other mental health professional.

GLOSSARY

acute
Lasting a short time.

antidepressant
A drug used to treat or prevent clinical depression that works by altering the function of brain neurotransmitters.

autism
A disorder characterized by problems with social development and communication.

bipolar disorder
A form of depression characterized by alternating mood changes from extreme high, manic states to extreme low, depressive states.

chronic
Lasting a long time.

diagnosis
The art or act of identifying a disease or condition from its signs and symptoms.

dysthymia (dysthymic disorder)
A lower-grade form of depression than major depression, in which symptoms are not completely disabling but are much longer lasting.

genome
A human's complete set of genes.

hormone
A chemical produced by an endocrine gland that travels through the bloodstream and controls body processes, including mood and behavior.

major depression (major depressive disorder)
The most serious and disabling form of depression, in which the person loses interest in activities and cannot function normally.

metabolism
Chemical processes inside the body that control energy use and storage.

minor depression
A form of depression in which symptoms last at least two weeks but do not meet the criteria of major depression; if untreated, it may develop into major depression.

neurotransmitter
A substance that transmits nerve impulses from one neuron to another.

schizophrenia
A chronic, disabling disorder characterized by the inability to correctly interpret reality, often resulting in hallucinations and disordered behavior.

ADDITIONAL RESOURCES

SELECTED BIBLIOGRAPHY

Cobain, Bev. *When Nothing Matters Anymore: A Survival Guide for Depressed Teens*. Minneapolis, MN: Free Spirit, 2007. Print.

Empfield, Maureen, and Nicholas Bakalar. *Understanding Teenage Depression: A Guide to Diagnosis, Treatment, and Management.* New York: Henry Holt, 2001. Print.

Parker, Gordon, and Kerrie Eyers. *Navigating Teenage Depression: A Guide for Parents and Professionals*. New York: Routledge, 2010. Print.

FURTHER READINGS

Monaque, Mathilde. *Trouble in My Head: A Young Girl's Fight with Depression*. Chippenham, Wiltshire, UK: Random, 2007. Print.

Parks, Peggy J. *Teen Depression*. Detroit, MI: Lucent, 2013. Print.

Schab, Lisa M. *Beyond the Blues: A Workbook to Help Teens Overcome Depression*. Oakland, CA: Instant Help, 2008. Print.

WEB SITES

To learn more about living with depression, visit ABDO Publishing Company online at **www.abdopublishing.com**. Web sites about living with depression are featured on our Book Links page. These links are routinely monitored and updated to provide the most current information available.

SOURCE NOTES

CHAPTER 1. HOW DO I KNOW IT'S DEPRESSION?

1. "Major Depression Facts." *Depression*. Depression Learning Path, 2001–2012. Web. 24 May 2013.

2. Marina Marcus, et al. "Depression: A Global Public Health Concern." *Depression: A Global Crisis. World Mental Health Day, October 10 2012*. World Federation for Mental Health, 2012. PDF file.

3. "Major Depression Facts." *Depression*. Depression Learning Path, 2001–2012. Web. 24 May 2013.

4. "Depression." *National Institute of Mental Health*. National Institutes of Health, 2011. Web. 20 May 2013.

5. John M. Grohol, PsyD. "DSM-5 Changes: Depression and Depressive Disorders." *Psych Central*, 2013. Web. 7 July 2013.

6. "Diagnosis of Depression: DSM-IV-TR Criteria for Major Depressive Episode and Major Depressive Disorder." *American Psychiatric Association*. American Psychiatric Association, 2000. Web. 24 May 2013.

7. "Depression." *National Institute of Mental Health*. National Institutes of Health, 2011. Web. 20 May 2013.

8. Maureen Empfield and Nicholas Bakalar. *Understanding Teenage Depression: A Guide to Diagnosis, Treatment, and Management.* New York: Henry Holt, 2001. 11–12. Print.

9. Ibid. 18.

CHAPTER 2. HOW DID I GET THIS WAY?

1. Maureen Empfield and Nicholas Bakalar. *Understanding Teenage Depression: A Guide to Diagnosis, Treatment, and Management.* New York: Henry Holt, 2001. 7–8. Print.

2. Ibid. 54–55.

CHAPTER 3. WHAT CAN HAPPEN TO ME?

1. "Effects of Bullying." *StopBullying.gov.* US Department of Health and Human Services, n.d. Web. 31 May 2013.

2. "Alcohol and Depression." *WebMD*, 2012. Web. 30 May 2013.

3. H. D. Abraham and M. Fava. "Order of Onset of Substance Abuse and Depression in a Sample of Depressed Outpatients." *PubMed.gov.* US National Library of Medicine, 1999. Web. 30 May 2013.

4. "Teen Suicide Is Preventable." *American Psychological Association.* American Psychological Association, 2013. Web. 31 May 2013.

5. "Teen Suicide." *The Ohio State University Wexner Medical Center.* The Ohio State University Wexner Medical Center, n.d. Web. 31 May 2013.

CHAPTER 4. FINDING OUT WHAT'S WRONG

None.

SOURCE NOTES CONTINUED

CHAPTER 5. TREATING DEPRESSION

1. "Depression." *National Institute of Mental Health.* National Institutes of Health, 2011. Web. 20 May 2013.

2. "Depression in Children and Adolescents Fact Sheet." *National Institute of Mental Health.* National Institutes of Health, 2011. Web. 20 May 2013.

CHAPTER 6. LIFESTYLE CHANGES AND ALTERNATIVE TREATMENTS

1. Lynette L. Craft, PhD, and Frank M. Perna, EdD, PhD. "The Benefits of Exercise for the Clinically Depressed." *The Primary Care Companion to the Journal of Clinical Psychiatry.* US National Library of Medicine, 2004. Web. 4 June 2013.

2. American Psychological Association. "10 Tips to Build Resilience." Psych Central, 2007. Web. 4 June 2013.

3. "Depression." *National Institute of Mental Health.* National Institutes of Health, 2011. Web. 20 May 2013.

4. Rena Freedenberg, ND. "Naturopathic/Holistic Treatment of Mild to Moderate Depression." *Natural Medicine Journal,* 2009. PDF file.

5. Kathleen Doheny. "Pets for Depression and Health." *Depression Health Center.* WebMD, 2012. Web. 22 May 2013.

CHAPTER 7. KEEPING PEOPLE IN YOUR LIFE

1. Hara Estroff Marano. "Depression: A Family Matter." *Psychology Today,* 1 Mar. 2002. Web. 5 June 2013.

2. Bev Cobain, RNC. *When Nothing Matters Anymore: A Survival Guide for Depressed Teens.* Minneapolis, MN: Free Spirit, 2007. Print.

CHAPTER 8. HELPING A DEPRESSED TEEN

None.

CHAPTER 9. YOUR FUTURE WITH DEPRESSION

1. Robert Johansson, MSc and Gerhard Andersson, PhD. "Internet-Based Psychological Treatments for Depression." *Expert Reviews*. Informa, 2012. Web. 7 June 2013.

2. Kathryn Rost, et al. "Managing Depression as a Chronic Disease: A Randomized Trial of Ongoing Treatment in Primary Care." *BMJ*. BMJ Publishing Group, 2002. Web. 7 June 2013.

3. "Future Treatments for Depression." *Ethiopian Review*. EthiopianReview.com, 8 Mar. 2010. Web. 27 May 2013.

INDEX

ABOUT THE AUTHOR

Carol Hand has a PhD in zoology. She has taught college biology, written biology assessments and high school science curricula, and authored more than a dozen young-adult books in science, health, and social studies. She has had firsthand experience with teen depression. Currently she works as a freelance writer of science books and online courses.